To find out more about the author and the work for business in Uganda, visit:

www.inachee.com

First published in the United Kingdom by Dickson Wasake.

Copyright © Dickson Wasake 2014. 2nd Edition.

Dickson Wasake asserts the moral right to be identified as the author of this work.

ISBN: 978-1-291-54471-8

Printed and bound by Lulu.com

All rights reserved. No part of this publication may be reproduced, stored in a retrieval system, or transmitted, in any form or by any means; electronic, mechanical, photocopying, recording or otherwise, without the prior permission of the publisher.

Dedications:

To all Ugandan entrepreneurs who strive to succeed, despite all the odds being stacked against you.

To my mother, whose entrepreneurial blood runs fast and deep within me and from whom I learnt the principle of keeping on fighting (to succeed) in the world of business.

Achieving Business Success (in Uganda)

10 simple but powerful principles to learn from

Dickson E Wasake, FCCA
(with Doreen Mwesigye)

2nd Edition.

Praise for Business Success (in Uganda)

It's a simple read but the message is very clear and the ideas are well articulated. The fact that it uses Ugandan examples helps and makes it easier to apply the advice.

Business challenges are unique for every community and country). I found all chapters to be appealing and useful but chapters 3 (*Secrets millionaires use to sell more*) and 4 (*Why businesses fail*) stood out.   *Moses Kihumuro, IT officer.*

Your book was excellent…. it came at a time when I needed such information. When is your next publication?   *David Were, Student, Makerere University.*

I have only managed a quick perusal, but I can already see that it is going to really help me, and my team. We are in the process of re evaluating our business strategy and processes in the day to day running of the company, so this lovely book comes in very handy. *Lorna Ssozi, Managing Partner, Ssozi, Wasolo, Alinda- Ikanza & Nagitta Legal Associates and Advocates (SWAN Legal).*

I'd really like to appreciate you for the book. It is not only informative & educating, it is also so easy to read especially for a person that is not book friendly. I loved the fact that real life examples are provided in addition to useful links and the sources of the information provided.

For a person that's looking to start business, I found the chapter about "why businesses fail" totally on point. I also like the way the book was written, the humour and grammar; it gives me a feeling that I am getting advice from a professional over a chilly weekend.

I could go all day explaining what I love about the book but I just have to thank you for the good work. Thank you Mr. Dickson Wasake. Only God can pay you for your work.   *David Nsubuga, Al Ain, Abu Dhabi.*

The book is good. Thank you. I liked most the evaluation tools in the Appendices, so helpful. I am using it as my hand book now.   *Rony Muganga, Businessman.*

I loved the book. It's very informative .The kind of book one needs if one wants to make a head way in business.   *Regina Owomugisha, Farmer.*

Table of Contents

What's my story?	2
How to read this book	5
Chapter 1: About Zari - a key lesson in Marketing	6
Chapter 2: Google, Face book and business success	8
Chapter 3: Secrets millionaires use to sell more	11
Chapter 4: Why businesses in Uganda fail	17
Chapter 5: What do lenders/financiers care about?	23
Chapter 6: Solving the bookkeeping problem	27
Chapter 7: Internal controls- be your own auditor	28
Chapter 8: Ensuring quality	30
Chapter 9: Just pay the taxes	33
Chapter 10: Which is the best sector for investment?	38
Appendix 1: 12 powerful words/phrases you MUST use in all your marketing material	42
Appendix 2: Business plan template	44
Appendix 3: Example internal control programme	48
Appendix 4: Example of exceptional customer care	66
About the author	68
Credits	69

What's my story?

a.k.a who am I to tell you about business success?

Accountants are sometimes referred to in a *"tongue in cheek"* fashion as being boring, so I will not make your will to live any worse with stories about how I became a Chartered Accountant (FCCA) or how I successfully completed my CPA Uganda exams, even after walking out of 2 exam papers before they finished, let alone about the double entry system of Debit and Credit.

I am however reminded of the story of a famous Bahamian poet friend of mine, Obediah Michael Smith. He once jokingly mocked me, asking, "What good could possibly come out of double entry?" In reply, I said (poetically of course):

The Caribbean express
On and on he goes,
Like the chook chook train
Trainloads of words, never broken, never derailed.

This book is the result of over 10 years of advisory experience.

It really started on the day when straight out of University I borrowed my big brother's ill-fitting suit (a green one at that), jumped onto a *boda boda* and headed off to the International Conference Centre (now the *Serena Hotel*) to make a presentation to the board of directors of an Event Management company (now one of the largest and most successful).

WHAT I DIDN'T TELL THEM is that the internal control concepts I was about to discuss were coming straight from my university "auditing 101" notes - concepts I had no real experience in.

WHAT I DIDN'T KNOW THOUGH was that the notes were pretty effective (and true)! I only found this out later when the company paid me (my first cheque) to review their internal controls.

Several years later, I am of course wiser (I hope) and have real practical experience. I have also been lucky to see first-hand how big and successful companies are run.

I started my career with the global accountancy firm *PricewaterhouseCoopers (PwC)* and one of the things they told us when we started is: "your career here is like taking the lift, while others take the stairs". It turned out to be true. I got to work with top notch clients in different sectors like *Coca Cola*, Bank of Uganda, *Unilever*, DFCU Group, *Kakira Sugar works* as well as UN and World Bank/IDB funded programmes.

In our work we did not just see the books of accounts but we saw the business strategies, the long term plans, and the corporate governance. We got to understand their industries; the things that made these entities successful and those that kept their top management worrying, wide awake at night.

I left Uganda and spread my wings in the Caribbean and then in the UK Channel Islands. My work continued to include clients in different sectors ranging from financial services (banks, insurance, and investments), real estate, agriculture, mining and including some listed on *AIM*, which is a part of the London Stock Exchange.

The highlight though for me was whilst doing assurance work for the Central Bank of Bahamas when the Governor of the bank (Wendy Craigg) commented on a report which I had authored:

"Never in my life have I seen a report like this."

A simple comment like that was all the assurance I should have needed that maybe after all, this was where I was best placed.... helping businesses find success....but it seems I was stubborn and didn't heed the call – immediately.

The idea to do advisory through the current firm Inachee started when a friend then sent me an email out of the blue: *"I have EUR 30,000, where should I invest?"*

Its then that I realised that there are several people who need advice, many who did not have the diverse and unique insights and experience I had gathered over the many years. I was genuinely able to help because I had seen both sides of the coin...as an entrepreneur (for example in a VOIP venture and as a director for a large and successful recruitment agency with over 2,000 staff/contractors). In addition I had acted as a financial advisor (in several countries).

But more importantly I felt I needed to give back something. Some will call it a God given calling... I knew in my heart that I had been "sent" to fulfil a purpose and my accumulation of significant experience from various industries in different parts of the world was so I could give back to the people of Uganda, alot of whom would otherwise have not been able to afford a top notch advisor (allow me just one second to brag and think I am one of those).......or many of them perhaps don't see the need for one, believing they can do it all on their own and save that precious money...

A lot of the FREE information we give is therefore born out of this "nagging" need to share and change Uganda, the world....And hence with Doreen Mwesigye (who has won a *"Woman Entrepreneur of the Year"* Award) and Joseph Walusimbi (an experienced sales and marketing professional) as my two other business partners (who shared a similar ethos), we set off... to help Ugandans to succeed...

Nevertheless, a lot of people, mock consultants or business advisors saying: "those who cannot do consult" or saying "it is a waste of time and money" but this cannot be further from the truth. Millions of companies have saved time and money and ACTUALLY MADE money following consultation with advisors.

A good saying I have heard was this: *"If you think hiring a professional is expensive, try an amateur"*…... I believe it is important to get the best.

Whilst for example as part of the senior management team in a "Top 10" accountancy practice in the UK, I once attended a marketing conference by Andy Bounds (who won *"Britain's Sales Trainer of the year"* award). As an advisor/consultant, he gave us new concepts (to me) on marketing like:

"Customers don't' care what you do, they care about what they are left with AFTER…"

Returning from the course, like a true disciple, I applied his simple yet effective benefit focused principles to a tender/proposal document I was spearheading for a large Trust company and Bank.

Our competitor at the time in the proposal was one of the largest audit firms in the world, a *"Big 4"* as they say in the accounting industry.

We won the job! What was more, we had previously been pitching for jobs of only £5,000 but this was worth £42,000 - our largest at the time.

So that's my story? What is yours?

How to read this book

As with any book, the best way to read it is sequentially, from the introduction to *chapter 1* and through to *chapter 10* and the credits as well (where I thank my team, the weather etc).

But sometimes it is not the case, especially the business owner/executive who is constantly busy and has to deal with many different things and hence might not have time to read the book from cover to cover, or might not (yet) be/she interested in certain topics.

I considered this when writing the book........

and so as much as possible, I made every chapter to be stand-alone. This means any chapter can be read without (mostly) reading any other chapter.

If you must read this book in bits, then I suggest you read the following:

- What's my story (which provides an introduction and background);
- Chapter 2: Google, Face book and business success;
- Chapter 3: Secrets millionaires use to sell more; and
- Chapter 4: Why Businesses in Uganda fail (with Doreen Mwesigye).

Next steps?

This book is about concepts and principles (including marketing strategies) that work. They have worked for many businesses all around the world, big and small (and I have seen this) and they can work in Uganda too (where we run a successful firm as well as have successful clients).

I hope you will find this book useful. I believe in these concepts and have seen them work. Whilst seemingly simple, do not be deceived, they work- powerfully.

Nevertheless, if you start reading and the ideas seem strange, that doesn't mean they are wrong. Just try them to see if they work. You have nothing to lose - particularly if all else you have tried has failed.

Once you have finished reading this book, if you are still interested in the work we do, then you can subscribe to the *"advanced thinking"* newsletter where many of these concepts are shared.

The link for subscription is at the website: www.inachee.com

And now..... To success (in Uganda)!

Chapter 1: About Zari – a key lesson in Marketing

Zari Hussein is a Ugandan socialite.

According to *Wikipedia*, the online encyclopedia, a socialite is someone who participates in social activities and spends a significant amount of time entertaining and being entertained…

Zari or *"the Boss Lady"* as she is commonly referred to seems to be ostentatiously wealthy and so is regularly featured in the Ugandan press; including when she purchased one of the few *Lamborghinis* at what I understand was over $280,000.

Her display of wealth, with no apparent "method to the madness" irked a blogger/writer called: "Degstar". Featuring on Friday April 12 2013 in an online edition of the magazine *chimpreports.com* he said (about her "waste of money"):

"…..*It'll be more worthwhile than just pissing that money away on sijui 'Tycoon Party', 'All White Party' and whatever else you got going on. And if these different enterprises succeed, which they should if you hire people like my cuz Dickson to help you out, well then, suddenly you'll find yourselves shareholders in lots of companies!*"

I didn't know about this all until I was looking at our website's performance via a website traffic analysis tool (*google analytics*). I noticed something strange. We were getting visitors from *chimpreports.com* (which I had never heard of until then).

It turns out, that Degstar had put a hyper link in his story, to our website and therefore readers of the story, curious to know about this "Cuz Dickson" who could help companies become successful were actually visiting our website. Over a 1 month period that we analysed the traffic, visitors from chimp reports (July-August) were spending on average 13 minutes!

Just for perspective, the average reader who visits a website spends 8 seconds before deciding to stay or move on. We know this because we also do online advertising and have compared the length of visits. The visits from *chimpreports* were much longer than those from our Google and Face book advertising.

It also turns out that Degstar happened to be one of our clients, blogging under the "Degstar" pseudonym. He had gone ahead to (of course without our knowledge) write this article which was now testifying to our work and the success of our firm (Inachee) in helping entrepreneurs succeed.

The point I am trying to make is this:

Businesses spend so much time telling customers about how good they are, blah blah… but in actual sense, customers are probably more swayed when <u>someone else</u> says this.

BUT how many Ugandan business websites, brochures, proposals or other marketing material do you know for example that have real testimonials, 3rd party endorsements, referrals and the like?

In our case, we were spending a fortune on advertising but in reality, 3rd party endorsements were having visitors stay much longer than through our own advertising.

A change to your business marketing strategy and material to include 3rd party endorsements (which you can probably get very easily) is one of the simplest yet powerful means of getting more customers and hence more sales.

But testimonials are not the only form of marketing a business can use. There are many others you can use. Some 3rd party examples of evidence you can use in your marketing include:

- Awards received
- Client Case studies
- Product Endorsements (including from celebrities like "*the boss lady*")
- Appearances in the press (e.g newspaper articles)
- Referrals from clients
- Customer reviews from independent sources (e.g websites. Critics, magazines)

Action point #1: Put this book down for a second and go find some testimonials. Start with your best customers.

Chapter 2: Google, Face book and business success

Pay per click advertising vs traditional advertising

Your customers are increasingly online.

- In Uganda, there were 6 million users on the internet by December 2012; this represented about 17% of the estimated 35m population.

- Of these users, about 1 million Ugandans are on *Face book* (January 2014) - compared to those reading newspapers, for example the *New Vision's* daily circulation is (only) about 34,000. Meanwhile many of these users are viewing on mobile devices.

- 50% of people on the internet are on *Face book* for half an hour – everyday while 48% of 18-34 year olds check *Face book* right when they wake up…about 28% check Face book on their smart phones before getting out of bed.

- *Google*, the world's largest search engine had total revenue in 2012 of $50 billion of which the bulk came from its advertising revenue via Ad words also called Pay Per Click (PPC). *Face book's* revenue for 2012 was about $5 billion of which the bulk also came from online advertising. Both companies revenues are growing by at least 30% from the previous years – on account of increased online activity.

The cost of taking out a quarter page black and white advert in the New *Vision* or *the Monitor*, the two most widely circulating newspapers is a minimum of Shs. 1,820,000 ($728) (at February 2013).

As mentioned above, the daily circulation figures of the *New Vision* are about 34,000 readers while for *the Monitor* this is about 24,000 (as per audited figures from *ABC*).

The challenge of Using newspapers for advertising though is of course you have no means of measuring how many people actually "see" your advert. I also do not know many small businesses (SMEs) which can afford this price – many larger companies can do this and newspaper advertising serves its purpose (we have advertised using the *New Vision* for example).

By comparison:

In 2011, according to the World Bank, 13% of Uganda's population (estimated at 34.5m) or 4.5m people had internet access.

The number of users had surpassed 6 million by December 2012, according to a Uganda Communications Commission (UCC) report: *"Status of the communication sector in Uganda."* This represented about 17% of the estimated 35m population.

Of these users, there are at least 1 million active *Face book* users in Uganda (January 2014 per *Face book* advertising stats). This means that for business, there are more internet users than those who read newspapers.

What is equally important to note is that according to a State of Uganda population Report 2012, Uganda has the youngest population in the world with over 78% being below 30 years of age.

This generation has grown up with the internet (or are more aware of it) and so a lot of your customers are online!

Your strategy should therefore definitely include *Pay Per Click advertising* (PPC). *Google* and *Face book* (amongst others) do this. What does it cost to advertise via pay per click?

It depends on your budget. You can set your budget as little as $1 a day. This works out at $30 a month. This is roughly Shs. 78,000 a month!

Now the advantage with Pay Per Click is that you can get reports that tell you exactly how many people clicked on your advert and visited your website. You can even tell how long they stay and what pages they visit. These tools are all provided free via *Google Analytics*, an application that enables you to assess how well your website is performing.

How about a website?

For your internet strategy to work especially pay per click, your website therefore needs to be professional looking, up to date and show case what sets you apart from the rest because the typical user who visits your website has about 8 seconds before they decide whether to stay or go.

Some experts even place this lower at 3 seconds!

It is easy to set up a website these days and if you are tight for cash, you don't need to pay a web designer. Many website hosting companies like yola.com, wix.com, 1and1.com provide what is called a Content Management System (CMS).

This is a web designing platform which is mainly a case of "drag and drop" of text, colours and designs and all other tools you need.

This means you can do all the designing yourself, as well as make regular updates to the website without knowing computer language (HTML, JAVA etc) or contacting a technical person. If you indeed need technical support, these hosting companies often have a knowledge database for free or free 24/7 IT support.

Does a good website matter?

In *American Beauty* the 1999 Oscar winning movie featuring Kevin Spacey, one of the characters had a memorable mantra:

"In order to be successful, one must portray an image of success at all times".

This is true in almost all aspects of doing business.

A doctor dresses and carries on like a doctor, and so is trusted to treat disease.

A lawyer dresses and carries on like a lawyer and so is trusted to litigate for their client successfully.

Their image and the way they are perceived therefore give their clients (or patients) the assurance that they are dealing with "the real thing."

How about a company, when clients first encounter you and your works, what impression do you give?

"Business is changing and potential customers are increasingly online. "

Their first image of your company is therefore from your website. Your website is the professional's equivalent of dress and business style. Your online strategy is therefore a critical part of your future growth.

How do you expect to have a chance of convincing customers that you are the best at what you do when your website for example:

1. Has spelling errors;
2. Has incomplete sections;
3. Is not up to date;
4. Looks like an amateur's work;
5. Contains links that do not work; or
6. Gives no indicator of why a client should choose your firm over millions of other similarly looking, and worded websites?

A company that strives to be successful should ensure that their website is at the forefront of their marketing strategy and not just relegated to the (nerdy) IT guy.

You should for example ensure you keep it regularly updated and communicate this to your clients (e.g via an email newsletter).

Action point #1 : Test Google and Face book pay per click advertising. You are potentially losing out on about 17% of your Ugandan customers who are online, including on their mobile devices/smart phones.

Action point #2: Develop a website. If you have one, review it to ensure it meets the guidelines above.

Chapter 3: Secrets millionaires use to sell more

Marketing tips from an accountant?

You are probably wondering why as an accountant, I am not telling you the "boring stuff" of double entry and how to cut costs and instead spending a lot of time on marketing?

Well you see the fact is this, the numbers in business don't lie. Businesses fail (and I will come to that in another chapter) because they didn't sell enough to cover their expenses.

I have seen it happen in plenty of businesses. The idea is brilliant but there is just not enough sales and so they keep cutting costs until they go out of business.

So for me, it is critical that clients get this marketing stuff right because more sales mean more chance of success – then you can hire as many "boring" accountants as you want.

A lot of accountants focus on the cost cutting stuff (which is important too), but what use is it to cut costs if you do not have the revenue in the first place to sustain your business? And the reality is this: If you are in business (rather than an NGO or charity or perhaps not selling a necessity like electricity), you have one primary aim: To sell more.

It is so difficult to get credit from banks and other parties in Uganda and as such selling more seems like the only key means of growing your business. It is why I am passionate about sales.

Now a lot the information I am about to provide comes from two of the world's leading marketing experts (BUT backed up by our experience). These experts are millionaires.

This stuff works

I am not providing it because it's from some "best seller" book or so called "marketing guru" but mainly because plain and simple: This stuff works.

It is working excellently for us. Our client portfolio is growing rapidly, every day, despite it being a very challenging economic environment.

It has worked for employers I worked with when we tested it (as I told you in the introduction). It can work for your business or organization as well. Hopefully instead of ignoring this, you will choose the "lazy" option which is to try these principles and save yourself loads of years of wasted effort of trial and error.

About these "sales" men.

Andy Bounds, who I mentioned previously, is half blind. His other "good eye" has limited vision such that he can't for example drive himself. His blindness is hereditary. He however won Britain's *"Sales Trainer of the Year"*. He explains that he is good because he had to explain things to his blind mother. He therefore sees things differently (no pun intended).

I have met Andy (twice) and I bought his best seller book: *The Jelly Effect*. I read his stuff because it works - it is simple, yet powerful. Andy typically charges £5,000 an hour for consultation. Yes you read right, £5,000 per hour!

The second is Chris Cardell. Chris has spent at least $1million on *Google* advertising and is considered one of the world's leading marketers. He helps his clients (many of whom are millionaires) achieve profits of up to 200%.

Until July 2013, I was a member of Chris's inner VIP members' club. Subscription is £56 a month. I read (and watched) his stuff because it works - it is simple, yet powerful.

P.S I still subscribe to Chris Cardell, not to his VIP inner circle club though, but another subscription that fits our needs more, especially as we have continued to evolve.

What are some of Andy's tips for selling more?

1. The AFTERs based principle.

"Clients want problem solvers not technicians" or put rather more bluntly:

'Customers don't care what you do. They care about what they're left with AFTER you have done it."

Why is this stuff very powerful?

When you focus on what a customer is receiving, i.e. the BENEFITS of your product/services (saving time, saving money, less stress) then you will stop focusing on stuff they don't really care about i.e. the features of your product (we are the best, the smartest, the fastest, the largest etc).

Key point:
When you focus on what your customers want, then instantly you become more interesting to them and they are more likely to come to you because you are solving their problems. They don't really care if for example you are the best lawyer in the world (though that helps) they really care that you can solve the problem with minimum fuss.

Action point #1: Think of your customers. What do they really want? What are the benefits of your product or service? After identifying this clearly, (think for example of 4-7 benefits) then work backwards to identify how your product/service meets their needs (i.e. benefits them)

2. How do you use your AFTERS to sell more?

There are two things your customers want when making a buying decision.

1. Their desired AFTERs and;
2. Absolute certainty that you can provide their AFTERS.

These are the only two things customers are interested in.

If they know with 100% certainty that they will get the AFTERS they require, they will buy.

This means traditional selling approaches like: "we were formed in 1993" "We are the best manufacturer of x" does not satisfy this criteria, and it does NOTHING to provide certainty that you can deliver a customer's afters.

To sell therefore you need to remember the ABC principle:

•**A**fters: Establish what the customers' AFTERS are (ask the customer what they want for example "what are you looking to achieve AFTER working with us?" "How would you judge this project a success?")

•**B**e Certain. State with certainty that you can provide these afters (this is a simple stage. First clarify that you understood and then say it, for example: "well I can definitely help you".
•**C**onvince. Prove that you can deliver those afters (this is where you have a bank of proof e.g. testimonials, client case studies BUT this time having restructured them to show how they meet the BENEFITS of the customer. You might already have much of the information (experience, case studies etc.) what you however need to *do is restructure it to first focus on what the client wants and then show how exactly you meet their AFTERS (needs).*

Action point #2: Review your sales material or the next proposal you do with the AFTERS hat on. Does it meet the above test? If not, then you need to restructure it from the perspective of the customer.

What are some of Chris's tips for selling more?

1. Make your customers loyal.

Try these two principles:

a. Mail them frequent, interesting and informative information (not necessarily selling to them). You can do this via a newsletter.
b. Position yourself as an authority. For example have a regular column in the newspaper.

2. Get your competitors to introduce you to their customers.

Sounds crazy but then hopefully you have a prospect list (potential clients). Despite your best efforts, you come to the conclusion that no matter what you do, some people are just not going to buy from you. These are the "non buyers".

You have spent a lot of money on them (and time) but they are worth nothing to you. Here's where you can be clever: Offer to trade your non buyers to your competitors, in return for their non buyer's list. Yes sounds crazy but these non buyers mean nothing to you so by swapping, you stand some chance of getting trade value from them.

3. Give to receive.

Instead of running your ads and other pieces with the intention of making an immediate sale, instead give something FREE (a free report, a sample-with no obligation) SO AS TO BEGIN A RELATIONSHIP.

4. Sell effectively, with integrity.

A sale is about service, not just selling. "You will get what you want in life, if you help other people get what they want."

5. Don't give up too soon.
Some statistics to probably scare you.

- 48% of sales people never follow up with a prospect
- 25% of sales people make a second contact and stop
- 12% of sales people only make three contacts and stop.

Only 10% of businesses make more than three contacts. This means you are losing a small fortune because:

- 2% of sales are made on the first contact
- 3% of sales are made on the second contact
- 5% of sales are made on the third contact
- 10% of sales are made on the fourth contact
- 80% of sales are made on the fifth to twelfth contact

6. Use your time wisely.

Not every prospect is equal. It sounds unfair or wrong but it's a true. The 80/20 rule is that 80 % of your business will come from 20% of your customers. It's a fact that some people will give you 100m and others will never amount to much.

Focus your attention on finding those potentials (the 20%) who will be the "best customers". Those who will give you a lot of money, repeatedly with minimum effort.

Special attention section: Permission based marketing

The continued rise of the internet as well as the increased use of cell phones means that customers are increasingly being bombarded with marketing information.

This means that the immediate sale rarely works.

Lead generation is therefore the way to go. What is Lead Generation?

In principle, the customer comes to you and they need more information. You provide it and then ask them (for permission) to start a relationship with you.

How do you provide this information? How about using SMS based permission marketing? Why? "SMS has a 100% read rate; you read every SMS you get".

As a lot of industry experts will tell you, mobile technology is the true African revolution. Your marketing strategy must therefore include bulk SMS services – low cost and yet effective.

How about e- mail? E mail marketing programmes like mailchimp.com allow users to send bulk e-mail at low cost (usually free up to a certain point say 500 subscribers).

Watch out though!

Radicati group research shows that 77% of marketers prefer e – mail marketing, but according to their other research on email, the average user receives 78 emails a day! In an 8 hour working day, this is about 10 emails an hour.

It means that the most important thing therefore is: **The Subject line.**

No matter how well written the body of your email, the recipient of your email must perceive an immediate benefit if you expect them to even open it and if not well written, 69% of users will delete your message or send it to SPAM before reading it.

Action point #3 For every SMS or email marketing (or other email you send) make sure the subject line (or 1st few lines) are going to make the recipient want to open it or ask for more information.

Action point:#4: Try to implement at least one of the above strategies (from Andy Bounds, Chris Cardell and Permission based marketing) per week and see how it works.

Then move on to the next. Within no time you will be implementing at least 6 sales strategies and growing sales by over 100%.

As a bonus, if you would like to know the 12 powerful words and phrases that you MUST use in your marketing, check out *Appendix 1*.

Chapter 4: Why businesses (in Uganda) fail

(With Doreen Mwesigye)

In 2012, Doreen Mwesigye was named "Woman Entrepreneur of the Year" in the "Top 100" Awards for the work with Job Connect Limited, of which is the principal shareholder. Job Connect has over 3,000 employees and contractors. Doreen is a principal at Inachee.

Businesses in Uganda and in particular small businesses, just like many start-ups elsewhere fail for similar reasons. A respected *New York Times* Article[1] on the subject gives the top 10 reasons for business failure as (summarised below):

1. The math just doesn't work. There is not enough demand for the product or service at a price that will produce a profit for the company.

2. Owners who cannot get out of their own way. They may be stubborn, risk averse, conflict averse.

3. Out-of-control growth.

4. Poor accounting. You cannot be in control of a business if you don't know what is going on.

5. Lack of a cash cushion.

6. Operational mediocrity. Repeat and referral business is critical for most businesses

7. Operational inefficiencies. Paying too much for rent, labour, and materials

8. Dysfunctional management. Lack of focus, vision, planning, standards and everything else that goes into good management

9. The lack of a succession plan

10. A declining market.

By comparison for Uganda, a study by Charles Tushabomwe- Kazooba *"Causes of Small Business Failure in Uganda"* [2] highlights some of the top 10 reasons as separated between external and internal factors to include (Summarised in table below as ranked from 1- 10):

---

[1] http://boss.blogs.nytimes.com/2011/01/05/top-10-reasons-small-businesses-fail/?_r=0

[2] http://www.africa.ufl.edu/asq/v8/v8i4a3.htm

Table 1: Why Businesses in Uganda fail

Rank	Internal	External
1		Taxation
2		Load Shedding(electricity)
3		Lack of Capital
4		Poor Market
5		High rent charges
6	Wrong pricing	
7	Negative cash flow	
8	Poor record keeping	
9	Domestic and family	
10		Delays in applications

IT IS INTERESTING TO NOTE THAT WHILST IN THE *NEW YORK TIMES* ARTICLE, ALL REASONS FOR FAILURE (EXCEPT No. 10) <u>ARE INTERNAL AND BLAMED ON THE SMALL BUSINESSES THEMSELVES, IN UGANDA, ALL THE TOP 5 REASONS ARE BLAMED ON EXTERNAL FACTORS.</u>

Which is correct? The author of the *New York Times* article rightly points out:

"*One of the least understood aspects of entrepreneurship is why small businesses fail, and there's a simple reason for the confusion: Most of the evidence comes from the entrepreneurs themselves.*

I have had a close-up view of numerous business failures —including a few start-ups of my own. And from my observation, <u>the reasons for failure cited by the owners are frequently off point</u>, which kind of makes sense when you think about it. If the owners really knew what they were doing wrong, they might have been able to fix the problem. Often, it's simply a matter of denial or of not knowing what you don't know."

I am therefore inclined to agree with the *New York Times* Article. Whilst it is true that Uganda has structural challenges that are not common in other developed economies where for example, electricity is a constant, roads are good etc, I can challenge you that in whatever circumstances, true entrepreneurs rise above the challenge, and find success.

The starting point is really the market. Will there be a market for your product? You need to know this. Seems obvious right?

I was once approached by someone who said he had a brilliant business idea. This was the idea:

An Airtime Scratcher Device.

The gentleman sent me an executive summary. One of the key statements was:

"Scratching an Airtime Card with human nails has always been challenging more especially to ladies. The Airtime Card Scratcher will be in form of, like a Card reader, it will be small, light and portable probably like a key holder. This will enable every person who has a mobile phone buy this device."

An idea is an idea and I couldn't discredit the gentleman. I therefore replied thus:

"Whilst people might want a machine that will help them to scratch the panel for airtime, the challenge here is, would they actually pay for the machine? If so, how much would they pay?

The alternative to scratching airtime cards with a machine is scratching with a money coin and so for your machine and idea to be viable, it would need to be sold for cheaper than Shs. 50 which is the lowest denomination coin that can be used."

The starting point therefore is to determine if there is a credible market for your concept and then once you are certain of it, develop your vision to do it better than the competition and voila, success, even if it is an airtime scratcher device!

Special section 1: Does treating people well matter?

A related aspect to considering business failure lies with the fact that in Uganda a lot of business entrepreneurs appear to treat their employees like disposable needles – to use and then throw away. "Labour is after all cheap and unemployment is high" they might reason. They therefore do not treat employees with value, and as such these employees either just don't care or they will sabotage the business.

Just how critical is it to treat employees well?

The Center for High Performance (CfHP) conducted a study of more than 3,000 knowledge workers around the world - the largest and most in-depth of its kind.

What did it find was common worldwide for high performing teams whether in Uganda or Antarctica i.e <u>regardless of their location, industry, sector or type of business?</u>

Characteristics present in High Performing teams

1. People in the group feel valued
2. It's fun to be part of the group.
3. The group makes use of the highest and best talents of its employees
4. The group works to retain the best people
5. People understand how their work fits the goals of the group
6. The group leader promotes high performance by his example

7. Important information about the state of the business is shared with everyone
8. The group continually looks for ways to work more efficiently
9. Information is freely exchanged in the work group
10. The work group turns problems into opportunities
11. New ideas are constantly sought
12. Learning is rewarded
13. The group adapts quickly to changes in the environment
14. New ideas are tried
15. Mistakes are seen as opportunities to learn

Action point #1: Perform a diagnostic of your business. Is one of the causes of failure identified above present:? If so, can you fix it?

Action plan # 2: Valuing people is critical for success. Is your team high performing? Ask them to take the survey here:

https://www.surveymonkey.com/s/CenterforHighPerformance

Special section 2: How to be successful (with Doreen Mwesigye)

Whilst this section primarily looks at why businesses fail – and therefore provides you with a blue print of what to avoid in order to prevent success, the key question someone might ask is this:

"But how exactly do you succeed in business?" For this I turn to Doreen Mwesigye.

Doreen has been my business partner since 2004.

In 2004 when Doreen wanted to start her firm, *Job Connect* (a company that helps large employers in Uganda, such as manufacturers by providing them with contract labour), she spoke to me about the concept. I helped her to do a "proof of concept" analysis which basically meant I looked at her initial ideas and gave her my views on areas she needed to look out for including a "sensitivity analysis" – an analysis to show how the business would survive, if for example, sales reduced 10% or costs increased 20%.

I helped her over the years with tax reviews, internal control reviews and other guidance. When it came to forming Inachee, she was the natural choice for business partner.

I share below with you her own words on success.

In my own words: 4 tips to becoming a Successful entrepreneur

(Doreen Mwesigye)

I started my business based on a 4 approaches I took way back in 2004.it is now 10 years down the road and it is fulfilling. I would say I was lucky that I was working for Enterprise Uganda, an organisation whose main mandate was to nurture Small and Medium size Enterprises (SMEs) and as the saying goes, the rest is history.

While running your own business certainly has its fair share of challenges, it can also be an extremely rewarding, lucrative and empowering pursuit.

Moneymaking opportunities are all around you if you have the knack for spotting them, though it can be difficult at first to develop a solid, marketable and interesting concept for a small business. Here are my 4 vital pointers that you could follow before you take the first step to starting your own business.

1. What is your Passion?

It's no good thinking you want to start a small business and then trying to come up with an idea on the basis of success of a friend or a business in the neighbourhood (copycatting)

Entrepreneurs who take this back-to-front route often fail because their "hearts" are not really in the project for the long haul. On the other hand, those who throw themselves into a lifelong passion or who realise a dream that's been nagging them for a while tend to flourish. Ask yourself honestly, if you have an idea you are so passionate about, could you devote the next 10 years of your life to it?

I know for example that there is money in managing a funeral home but how many of you have the heart to do forecasts that include the dead!!! And don't forget to consider if starting a small business is really for you – if you're not interested in the all-or-nothing entrepreneurial world, you may find it hard to get your idea off the ground and so it might be easier to stick to your employment.

2. Problem solver

All businesses, big and small, have one thing in common – they provide a service or product that solves a problem. Mineral water processors solve the problem of drinking water; market shoppers solve the problem of busy people who don't want to go the market; wedding planners solve the problem of too-much-to-do, not-enough-time. So, ask yourself –what problem do you want to solve? And once you've defined it, ask if there is a problem at all. How many people have this problem? Can they solve it for themselves, or do they need help? Is anyone else trying to solve the problem? Answering these questions will give you a good sense of whether the idea is worth pursuing at all, and what niche or group it would be aimed at.

Problems are easily spotted right from your home, where you cannot get good bread, to house helps, to the transport system, to lack of food at workplaces.

So, start spotting the problems even when you think it is too big to solve like the potholes.

3. Create a bathroom mantra

A bathroom Mantra is a 1 minute summary and explanation of your idea. If you were to meet someone on a busy path, how would you describe your business in one minute?

Ideally, your pitch should include one sentence that fully summarises your offering, and then a bit of extra detail if there's time. For example:

"Job Connect will provide companies with quality and on time semi-skilled labour" or:

"My salon will provide services to only children - plaiting and shaving."

Creating a pitch provides you with a lot of clarity on your concept. If you can't summarise your idea in a sentence, then it probably needs a bit more defining.

4.Research

There is absolutely no substitute for performing thorough research before you even consider launching a business around your idea. You need to gather information on how many local businesses already fill a similar need, whether anybody is experiencing the problem you want to solve, what your target market looks like and how much somebody would be willing to pay, among other things. The advantage of this is that you may end up with a very different and much better idea.

You can conduct research in a number of ways. The internet– spend time searching for keywords and phrases related to your business and see what comes up. Look at local business.

Don't forget to talk to people – canvass you friends for their opinions, and speak to people in your target market to see whether they would pay for the sort of service or product you want to offer, do whatever it takes to gather information about the potential of your idea. Every minute spent researching is an investment in your future.

Otherwise best of luck in your endeavor and remember – success is hard work, but it pays.

Chapter 5: What do lenders/financiers care about?

In business, the reality is that at one point, you will most likely need to apply for a loan or seek financing from a 3rd party.

Assuming your idea is viable and you have adequate security (if looking for a loan) then there are a number of things to know about from the lenders' perspective, because like in the *"Art of War"* a book on military strategy, author Sun Tzu says: *"Know your enemy."*

When we started featuring on our sister website a regular series on alternative sources of finance, we looked at the requirements of some of the following:

Table 2: Some providers of finance in Uganda (August 2013)

Type of financier	Examples of firms we researched on
Venture capital firms P.S This is funding available *primarily for startup companies*. The venture capitalist usually takes a % of shares (instead of collateral) and expects to exit in say 5-7 years from the company.	• Fanisi Capital • Acumen Fund • Accion Venture Lab • TBL Mirror Fund • Mara Launch Fund
Private Equity Firm P.S This is funding available primarily for *established business* to grow to the next level. The private equity fund also takes a % of shares or might also offer debt or a combination of both.	• Catalyst Principal Partners • Jacana Partners • Emerging Capital Partners • Pearl Capital Partners
Grant provider	• United States African Development Foundation (USADF) • GEF Small Grants Programme • US Embassy
Lender (e.g development bank)	• Uganda Development Bank • Grofin Uganda

Source: www.inachee.biz

A number of trends emerged and so I believe it is necessary to include these because as long as you have a successful business and are serious about success, more often than not you will need to seek a loan or other form of 3rd party financing beyond your internal means.

The following are the key considerations from the lenders we researched on:

Corporate governance

First things first. What is corporate Governance? Put simply:

"It is the process by which the company's management is being monitored by someone else." It is the process of for example having a board of directors to set the framework and to whom management are accountable.

Why is this stuff important for the lenders/financiers?

In many cases, there is a direct correlation between companies failing (failing to take off, making losses, winding up) and not implementing proper checks and balances.

Besides these lenders themselves are often supported by institutional investors, pension funds, government bodies, international lenders (like IMF) and other backers who need to be sure that the entity they are investing in is running the business properly with proper checks and balances like: board of directors meetings, a board with an independent non executive, regular accounts and regular internal control checks.

All the largest and most successful companies have strong corporate governance and so likewise these lenders expect that before they part with their hard earned money, you will have this in place.

Audited accounts

It goes without saying that typically for you to get 3rd party funding, they will expect to see your books of accounts, as independently reviewed by an auditor (a special type of accountant).

Why is this stuff important?

The lenders are investing their money (or other people's money) so they need to reasonably satisfy themselves that you are giving them the "real deal". Many of these firms will expect at least 3 years of audited results (hopefully profitable). The more reputable your auditor, the higher the chance that they will take you at your word.

Scalable market

I have spoken about the market before but a lot of these guys, say like the venture capitalist firms are looking to make a profit from their shares in your company, should it turn out to be the next big thing (like say *MTN, Google or Face book*). They want to get say 5 times their investment and to get this kind of return; they need to be sure that your market is big. Say the East African Market.

Scalable basically means that if the concept/idea works say in Uganda, then it can be repeated/rolled out in say Kenya, Tanzania, Southern Sudan and Rwanda. For example like Mobile Money.

Team

Again for firms whether it is the venture capitalists (who invest in start up/early growth companies) to private equity firms (which invest in more established companies), it is critical that the team is experienced, ambitious and has vision to implement its strategy.

It means that if you are to therefore put together your business plans, you need to clearly put together a strong balanced team with sufficient experience. One that will convince lenders that the idea will work successfully and the team knows what it's doing (and where its going).

Ethics and social impact

Financiers are increasingly conscious about whether the company will act responsibly. There is nothing that damages a company's fortunes like bad publicity from unethical practices (such as land grabbing) and in this day and age, information travels very fast via *Twitter, Facebook* and other social media platforms.

It is therefore important that your business plans can clearly show how your plans will first not do harm to the community but will more importantly be impactful – in your local community.

Action point #1: Why not check your business plan against our template included for you **Appendix 2**.

Special section: The rise of the Ugandan Diaspora lender

A 2012 UN report and Bank of Uganda figures estimates show that "Diasporas" have been transferring over $700m annually to Uganda. A figure that has been increasing by 10% each year and expected to reach $1bn in 2014!

This contribution in 2013/2014 is estimated to be about 25% of Uganda's Annual Budget, 6% of Gross Domestic Product (GDP) and its now higher than Foreign Direct Investment (FDI) i.e money from foreign investors.

It has also surpassed the earnings from traditional cash crops like coffee – and mind you Uganda is Africa's largest exporter (2013).

Who or what exactly are the Diaspora?

Diaspora is a term used to refer to persons with a similar heritage or homeland, but who are no longer living there. In Uganda, these persons are commonly referred to as *"Ugandans abroad", "Nkuba Kyeyo" or "Summers".*

The profile of "Kyeyos" has however changed over the years so you should be careful when using the phrase.

These persons are no longer predominantly doing menial jobs (hence the original "Kyeyo" phrase). Infact, about 2/3 of all remittances are actually from highly skilled persons.

What's more, in 2012, the bulk of the remittances actually came from next door Kenya, not US or UK as was the case traditionally (though these latter two remained key contributors).

What do the Diaspora have to do with lending?

Many Ugandans abroad are consistently looking for opportunities to invest in Ugandan businesses. They after all already have the "country at heart" and they already understand "how things work".

They go further; they combine this understanding of Ugandan with best practice learnt from their experience abroad.

The combination of the understanding in Uganda combined with experience from abroad means that they can be an excellent source of lending.

It means that businesses that seek financing should consider seeking funds particularly from Diasporas, who might be more likely to lend than many traditional alternative lenders.

But you need to know that Diaspora will probably scrutinize your plans more, they after all already understand.

And what's more they may expect you to present the information via internet – after all many of them using internet about 81% of the time (based on usage from the US and UK).

Do you know a Diaspora person or organisation who can support your plans? Do not ignore them – they are a powerful source of finance, but you need to put yourself in their shoes to understand.

Chapter 6: Solving the bookkeeping problem

I am going to keep this chapter short and sweet. The benefits of having accounting records are numerous and in addition to the benefit I mentioned for the lenders (as in the previous chapter), there are other benefits including that the information can provide insight into your cash flows, your pricing and your profitability. Hence enabling you to make informed business decisions.

There is a catch as well; you need the records for tax and legal purposes.

The *Income Tax Law of Uganda* and the *Companies Act* oblige you to keep a reasonable record of your transactions.

Accounting records are the lifeblood of any business and so you ignore them at your own peril. But the problem is this – Many businesses hate the process of maintaining records, or they just don't see the benefits (and ignore the legal requirements).

If you do not like bookkeeping and accounting, or if you do not have the skills or the time, then just do one thing and save yourself the time and concern: Outsource it!

The logic particularly if you are smaller business is that it is much cheaper to outsource this function to an accountancy firm than to have a full time in house accountant.

Unless your business needs daily entries, then you do not need to employ a full time accountant. Have one to visit you say weekly, monthly or quarterly. Many accounting firms (with several qualified accountants) would charge as little as Shs. 300,000($120) a month to do your bookkeeping.

This is certainly much cheaper than hiring a full time accountant/bookkeeper. A qualified accountant by comparison costs about Shs. 1,500,000 ($600) a month.

With "cloud accounting" options now available, it is possible for your bookkeeper to maintain your records online (securely) and you can access them anytime, anywhere. Some cloud accounting providers (January 2014) include: *Quickbooks online, Kashoo Xero*

The Ugandan accounting institute (ICPAU) has a list of accounting firms if you need a place to start to find a firm to whom to outsource this role.

P.s: You should however know that just because you have outsourced it (hence delegated responsibility) you shouldn't give up your involvement. Challenge your accountant to explain in "plain English" what the accounts mean to be sure that you understand what is presented and the implications for you.

Chapter 7: Internal controls- an introduction

a.k.a how to be your own auditor.

So we are back to where I began my career... Internal controls.

What did I share with that large and successful event management company that made them choose to hire me to implement my suggestions?

Patience….. I will get to that but before I do, what exactly are internal controls?

If corporate governance is "the process by which the company's management is being monitored by someone else." Then corporate governance sets the framework or the foundation for internal controls.

Internal controls is therefore the detailed systems of checks and balances including of staff and management (or by staff and management) to ensure that the entity continues to run smoothly.

Internal controls is stuff like the business owner counting stock every month to ensure that it is correct and accurate and that the store clerk has been doing the right thing.

It is obvious that the system of internal controls put in place depends on the size and complexity of the organisation. Some of the larger clients I dealt with for example had whole internal audit departments with several staff who looked at the control environment of the company.

Large banks for example even have software that can automatically detect anomalies of when controls are not working (as well) as they should.

A good internal control system covers areas like:

- **Corporate governance** – Is there a board that is running the company efficiently?
- **Sales and debtors** – can sales be unrecorded and debtors remain uncollected for long?
- **Purchases and creditors** – Can purchases be inflated and creditors not paid?
- **Fixed assets** – is there a fixed asset register to track assets?
- **Bank accounts** – Can cash be taken out of the bank account without authorisation?
- **IT and Insurance Risks**- are all assets adequately protected or insured?

I am sure you can see how much fun the above areas are! Anyway all joking aside, for a company that is growing, this stuff is serious and however boring it is, you need to be aware of it. If you don't like it, like the accounting/bookkeeping: outsource internal control checks.

If of course you are interested, or want to know what I shared with that company, I attach in *Appendix 3* a sample internal control programme (I have tweaked it from the years of experience). Go on, see for yourself what makes accountants (or auditors) hot and excited!

In all seriousness though, I strongly urge you to see the programme in *Appendix 3*, use it as a checklist to see for yourself if your business meets these minimum standards, if it doesn't then you are probably going to be in a lot of trouble.

Chapter 8: Ensuring quality

Fast food restaurant *Kentucky Fried Chicken (KFC)* opened its doors in Uganda in late 2013 and boy or boy was there a lot of social buzz about it. Everyone was exclaiming about the Shs. 99,000 bucket of chicken and some were even taking "selfies" (a photo taken by yourself, usually on a phone camera) at *KFC*. This reminded me of something.

One of the best business books I have read is Michael Gerber's best seller, the *E- Myth revisited: Why Most Small Businesses Don't work and what to do about it.*

He says fast food chain *McDonalds* (similar to *KFC*) is a small business. He went on to explain that *McDonalds* is really the *"largest small business in the world"* what he meant is that in essence, every *McDonalds* is run by different business owners ("franchisees").

Technically he is correct. In the book he describes why *McDonalds* is successful. One of the reasons is because its founder, a man called Ray Kroc set out to solve the franchise problem by thinking of how a small business could be run "by the lowest possible capable person".

This he did by having a detailed system of processes and procedures. These processes and procedures are so prescriptive that even the least educated or experienced person (no offence to *McDonalds'* employees) can run it, simply by following the instructions.

The logic applies to any other typical small (or big) business as well. If you put in place policies and procedures for what you do, then you can consistently produce a good/service at the same level of quality (whichever way you and your industry define or understand quality) and this can be done by the "lowest possible capable person". It doesn't mean that anyone can wake up today and go the hospital to treat patients but it means that in that business, the least capable can do the job required (for example a junior doctor following instructions to diagnose patients).

<u>The business can even (and should) run without you.</u>

Every successful company has standards, policies and procedures that are applied and followed (in many cases with military precision). This consistency is the solution to ensuring consistency, and hence quality as <u>perceived by the customer</u>.

Quality is quite intangible and cannot be easily described but the logic is that if you have repeat customers then presumably they are returning because they are satisfied with your product/services. This means they are likewise satisfied inherently with the quality of your product/service.

Logically it follows therefore that if you consistently deliver your product/service at the same "level" and keep your customers returning, then you are offering a quality product!

The solution therefore to ensuring quality is to deliver a consistent product/service that meets your customers' needs every time, in the same way.

And *McDonalds* does that well!

So if you think about it, for their customers (like me) they offer a quality product because every time I go to *McDonalds*, the *Big Mac* burger tastes exactly the same as the last time I was there, whether at 9.00 am or 9.pm, whether it was 5 years ago, or just the night before – that is quality because (and this is critical) as a *McDonalds* customer (not for example a *Burger king* or *KFC* one) they meet my needs - in the same way, every time.

In order to ensure quality, the solution therefore is to put in place policies and procedures to guide your staff in delivering the exact same product/service as they did yesterday, last year etc (you get the point).

A perception of quality is down to even the simple things…. Like sending documents.

If for example you deal with clients and regularly send them documents like invoices, letters and correspondence, do me one favour: make sure that you check (and/or have a system to check) those documents once, twice and if possible by a second person.

Why? Customers or others perceive quality from simple things and it is often attention to detail that separates a good quality firm/company or individual from an average one. A spelling mistake, forgetting to check that the document has included the relevant details the customer asked for and the like are more critical than you think.

In this day and age, with so many alternatives, you might only get one chance to impress. Don't blow it!

If you are a small entity or a one person team, start by ensuring your spell check function is turned on. Secondly, consider having a colleague (even one unconnected with your function) to check documents, products or even reports to give them that "sense check."

Imagine you are the head of procurement and you receive an invoice from a supplier and they have forgotten to include their VAT details or a current telephone number or got the quantities wrong. Does that instill confidence in their ability to delivery?

If you do not have the internal technical capability to review documents (say accounting records or legal documents), or products then outsource this expertise but do not put the reputation of your company on the line. There are a few things that separate good firms/individuals from the average ones.

Quality delivery is one of those.

For a small firm, besides the system of controls and checks I mentioned, the easiest means of ensuring quality control is through having a segregation of duties.

This means having someone independently checking your work, your products etc. You will be surprised at how many mistakes or errors can be picked up by this second review process.

If you don't have internal capacity, enter into a contract or arrangement where say you outsource this to an experienced "reviewer" and you pay them a retainer or a per piece rate. If it's a part time role, the extra money as well as a chance to use their expertise will benefit all.

Special section: Customer care and quality.

As you may probably know, in business there is what is called the "80/20" rule which in summary is that 80% of your business comes from 20% of your customers. these are usually repeat customers and so this is the reason a quality system is so important - your customers (the ones who bring the most money) expect the same level of quality from day to day. Get it right and you will be laughing all the way to the bank.

Businesses that excel create what is called a "value proposition". A set of unique benefits that they alone can provide to customers.

A business in any sector (yes any sector) can develop a value proposition that will always leave customers with a "wow" factor. One of these customers might be what Malcolm Gladwell in his famous book *"the tipping point"* called "connectors" i.e., those people who have a wide network of casual acquaintances by whom they are trusted, often a network that crosses many social boundaries and groups.

These connectors if impressed will probably bring in many more customers than any other customers (again the 80/20 rule works here i.e the connector probably brings in 80% of customers).

Action point #1 : Why not start maintaining a system where you can track each of your customers to see whether they are repeat or one off. Once you do so, you will be surprised to note that the 80/20 rule applies. This should enable you to put in place a system to ensure that you give these customers exceptional customer service – they are after all your life line.

In *Appendix 4* I set out for you 1 story that gives an example of excellent customer care.

Chapter 9: Just pay the taxes

When I originally wrote this article and sent it to our subscribers, the title of the email was:

"Just pay the $% taxes".*

One of the subscribers (a regular at that) immediately sent the newsletter to trash as "spam" and thus my mail delivery company automatically unsubscribed him from the newsletter. I suspect he didn't even read the main text of the article.

If he had read further, he would have noted that the $%* I meant was "bloody" meaning, "Just pay the bloody taxes". I will not question where his mind raced to when I sent the article but oh well…

The reality is this; no one likes to pay tax, or if they do, it is the bare minimum. It is not only in Uganda that people don't want to pay taxes, its universal, but I think it is a bit extreme in Uganda.

A culture of non compliance?

One of my friends asked me to call him one Saturday morning.

He was worried and wanted tax advice on how his business, which I estimated had more than Shs. 200m ($80,000) in sales, could continue to fly "under the radar" meaning- by not paying even one cent of tax! Not PAYE, Not VAT, Not Corporate tax, not WHT. He wanted to pay nothing!

I was pretty mad at him (mainly for waking me up early) so of course I told him:

"Just pay the bloody taxes"

His calm response (as if as a matter of fact) was:

"I cannot Pay As Yoweri Eats (PAYE).

This latter statement being a jest aimed at H.E the president (Yoweri Museveni for those from outer space) and the endemic corruption in Uganda which supposedly depresses him and makes him not pay taxes. I agree we have major issues where there appears no "value for money" but that doesn't mean we run from responsibilities.

In addition to the flagrant disregard to proper business ethics, I cannot deal with our Ugandan hypocrisy as a whole.

You know how we learnt it?

From the very polite Baganda who will invite you to a meal as you pass by the roadside saying:

"Jangu tulye" (come and let's eat) ……….

DON'T FALL FOR THIS! In actual sense, proper etiquette (or pretence if you prefer) dictates that you are supposed to turn it down (even if your stomach is rumbling). What you must say "Ugandan style" is:

Nva kulya kati! (I have just finished eating!)

Oh where was I? Yes, hypocrisy. We are a nation of mostly Christians (over 80%) but then the majority of us have <u>elaborate measures we take to dodge taxes.</u>

Actions speak louder than words and so we seem to be telling the world:

"Praise the Lord (ah), my brother, I have a testimony, with the God given wisdom, today I dodged taxes of Shs. 100m, halleluiah!"

Does that even make sense! If I recall, isn't it the good Lord himself who set out one of the principles of Christians and taxes:

"Give unto Caesar what belongs to Caesar?"

Do Christians not know that:

"Caesar" can be a cruel man and will take your shirt and your tunic too?

I just cannot understand why Ugandans do not have a compliance culture. Always trying to "cut corners" <u>until the corners cut them.</u>

The heat in the kitchen is only beginning to go up….

If you really want to "cut corners", please do me a favour, at least cut them from a point of knowledge!

"Your enemy is roaming around like a lion, seeking who to devour"

For the uninitiated, the "corner cutting" or "dodging" I am speaking about is tax planning and tax avoidance mechanisms, which are legal (or acceptable) compared to tax evasion, which is illegal.

And the enemy I refer to is not the nice, decent and polite folks at Uganda Revenue Authority (URA), BUT rather the "enemy" is the Income tax law. The "enemy" I refer to is the shortfall in Uganda's tax revenues….This short fall can change very easily, for example if the donors turn off the taps of aid…… This means we will have no option but to raise the revenue for our domestic needs, by ourselves.

There is nothing that brings about innovation like desperation…. URA will get smarter as the heat of revenue shortfall is turned up, that I can promise you.

A prime example is the November 2012 scandal in the Office of the Prime Minister (OPM) which resulted in Britain, (followed or preceded by other donor countries) suspending aid of over $42m following claims that OPM staff funneled $12.7m of money for aid programmes into private accounts.

With the global economic crisis continuing, this scrutiny of use of foreign aid funds and indeed tax leakage continues....

During 2013, large billion dollar multinational corporations like *Google, Apple, Starbucks and Amazon* have all been under fire about their tax affairs because the US taxman needs money!

The US even introduced a complex law called FATCA in order to deal with tax compliance by US citizens anywhere in the world. The resultant effect of this far reaching law is that countries around the world (led by their financial institutions) need to submit information on foreign accounts held by U.S citizens.

EVEN SWITZERLAND, which for hundreds of years has been known for its secretive banking laws is being made to "cough up" money hidden in its accounts and pay it over (to the US for example). It is even changing some aspects of its banking laws on account of these changes.

Once they finish dealing with the big fish, they will turn to the smaller fish including tax havens and this will trickle down to Uganda. And don't think URA isn't watching.

The message from all the above is this:

"The times they are a changing"

[As made famous by Bob Dylan in a similarly titled song in 1964]

Is there any good that ever came out of tax compliance?

This is not a message meant to preach *"fire and brimstone pouring out of the sky"* but rather it is show that in these tough times, the benefits of compliance outweigh the cost and headache.

The whole point of this article is to say, there is hope!

You can arm yourself with tools to succeed in business, even whilst complying.

Benefits of compliance (including accounts and tax monitoring)

Business intelligence. Having proper records of accounts means that you can analyse how your business is performing and therefore develop quick strategies to succeed, including to assess why your business might be failing. You really cannot succeed in business without knowing how well you are performing (or why you are failing) and records are the lifeblood of business.

Access to cheap loans and financing for expansion. You can get access to better loans and sources of finance with proper records and evidence of compliance.

You see all those guys with the "big bucks" (Venture capitalists, private lenders, private equity and other providers of finance) as I mentioned in *Chapter 5* are themselves sponsored by large corporate investors, wealthy individuals, government money, pension funds etc and so it is critical that they show that the money has gone to companies that are "good corporate citizens".

Usually they want to see your historical records (such as board minutes and tax certificates). Getting a loan from a bank at 22% interest per annum is certainly much cheaper than the money lenders who charge 15- 20% per month, that amounts to interest of at least 180% per annum!

Access to tax planning tools. Once you start maintaining proper records, you can start seeing how much you are spending and start seeing how to save on your tax burden through various tax planning strategies including the following examples (based on the Income Tax Law as per 2012):

PAYE (the real Pay As you Earn)

- Instead of paying meals allowance, provide meals to all staff. This is tax deductible.
- Instead of paying medical allowance, provide medical insurance. This is tax deductible.
- Instead of paying all as salary, why not pay part of it into a private pension scheme. This is tax deductible.

Corporation tax

- Consider assessing whether you qualify for certain deductions such as: first year allowances, start up allowances, bad debts allowance, training allowance, management charges paid. All these are allowable deductions that can, with proper planning reduce your tax liability.
- Also any losses you make in business during a year are tax deductible. This means you can "carry them forward" to the next year (or years) when hopefully you are profitable. This means, they offset any future profits you make until they are fully utilized/exhausted. There is a silver lining to making losses!

What if I refuse to see the benefits of compliance?

If the benefits of compliance don't sway you, then there is the reality that the Income Tax Law imposes penalties on for example not maintaining proper records and giving false information to a tax officer.

It also gives a lot of discretionary powers to URA, to for example turn up at your premises, without prior notice, and taking any records, equipment (such as computers) as they think fit are necessary to help them assess tax payable.

Business in Uganda is challenging enough as it is and so if you really want to save yourself the headache of taxes:

Just pay the %$* taxes!

*P.S: If the style of the chapter has been a bit "heavy", I hope unlike my subscriber (the one who unsubscribed) you will realise that it has partially been written in a "tongue in cheek" style. According to Wikipedia (which I love): "**Tongue-in-cheek**" is a phrase used as a figure of speech to imply that a statement or other production is humorously or otherwise not seriously intended, and it should not be taken at face value.*

Chapter 10: Which is the best sector for investment?

This book wouldn't be complete without me telling you about the *"Best Sectors list"*.

As you recall, I told you in the introduction that the work we are doing was borne partially as a result of the need to help other investors get relevant information before going into a sector.

To solve the problem, I sought inspiration from the *BBC* car show *"Top Gear"*. What I wanted to do was, like *Top Gear*, which ranks cars on the basis of fastest lap time as driven by *"the Stig"*, rank businesses in Uganda on the basis of a certain common method, but which one?

I settled on Return on Investment (ROI) in years. Why? Ugandans like "quick returns", "quick deals". A list which showed them how to make the most money in the quickest time was a real winner.

I am yet to know why we like this *"get rich quick"* thing but oh well…

So which is the best sector for investment? You ask.

I wouldn't be a consultant if I didn't tell you that:

"It depends"

My business partner, Doreen Mwesigye, who has won *"Woman Entrepreneur of the Year"* in the Top 100 awards and also run *Job Connect* a company which at last count had over 2,000 employees/sub-contractors and operating in Uganda, Southern Sudan, Tanzania and Rwanda thinks that one of the most important factors to consider before venturing into any sector is:

Passion.

In her own words (also in Chapter 4) she says:

"It's no good thinking you want to start a small business and then trying to come up with an idea on the basis of success of a friend or a business in the neighbourhood (copycatting)

Entrepreneurs who take this back-to-front route often fail because their hearts are not really in the project for the long haul. On the other hand, those who throw themselves into a lifelong passion or who realise a dream that's been nagging them for a while tend to flourish.

Ask yourself honestly, if you have an idea you are so passionate about, could you devote the next 10 years of your life to it?"

There are of course several other factors to consider including for example risk appetite (some investors like risky stuff, others are more conservative)

BUT… after all is said and done, so which is the best sector??

It is (drum roll)…. Forestry !

" Really? But trees take 15 years to grow!" You are probably protesting.

Yes, agreed but the return when annualized means you get back your investment in the equivalent of only about 2-3 months.

The top 5 sectors as per our ranking (January 2014) is:

Table: Top 5 sectors for investment in Uganda

Rank	Sector	Return on investment (Years)	Startup capital required (UGX)
1.	Forestry	0.21	22m
2.	Mushrooms	0.23	4.4m
3.	Fruits and vegetables	0.26	13.5m
4.	Property Management	0.6	35m
5.	Pharmacy	0.88	43m

To find out how we rank the sectors as well as the other sectors we consider, visit our website to find out how we did it:

www.inachee.com

Special section: What do Ugandans care about?

If you do not believe in our rankings, there is another way to think of which are the best sectors for investment in Uganda. Use trend analysis.

Google, the world's largest search engine on an annual basis analyses what the world searches for. Its latest (released January 2014) is: *"Google Zeitgeist 2013"*. I reviewed this information, like I did in 2012.

So what are Ugandans searching for, and how can these be turned into investment opportunities?

1. Football. . Like in 2012, football was the no.1 searched for item by Ugandans in 2013. Top searched websites included *livescore.com* and *xscore.com*.

How do you turn this into a money making opportunity?

It would seem that the biggest opportunity is sports betting/gambling tailored to Uganda (for example by accepting mobile money). Ugandans were in 2013 asking Google: *"How to bet"*.

I agree gambling is a social vice (just like alcohol and cigarettes) – and so this idea is not "every one's cup of tea" but some of the largest tax payers and employers in Uganda are beer companies – *Uganda Breweries* and *Nile Breweries* and the Tobacco company – BAT.

This activity should therefore be heavily regulated to protect vulnerable people like children.

Another opportunity, if gambling is not appropriate for you is specialty sports shops that not only sell the traditional football Jerseys but related items like sports autobiographies, mugs, car stickers, sports stars' face masks (for parties) and similar sports items and memorabilia.

2. Entertainment (and social media). Ugandans are big on entertainment, but this is changing towards online/social media. "Facebook" was the top search in 2013. Meanwhile on *Youtube* (2nd largest search engine after *Google*), top searches included: "Anne Kansiime", a comedian; *Choti Bahu* (Indian soap opera) as well as for "Ugandan Music".

In 2013, the most searched for person was an entertainer (not a politician), it was H.E. Bobi Wine! Other top searches were Chris Brown, Rihanna, Bebe Cool and Konshens.

Ugandans are increasingly using online tools like *Whatsapp* (a messaging service), *Waptrick* (a portal for free information such as MP3 songs, movies, games) and *Tubidy* (a mobile video search engine).

How do you turn this into a money making opportunity?

Websites with targeted advertising. Google's *Ad words* and Facebook offer targeted advertising. What this means is that you can choose your adverts (e.g of a website to download Ugandan music, movies, games or Ugandan comedy) to only show to Ugandans.

Don't ignore online sales using *PayPal* for example. This is important because there is a (forgotten) group who use the internet – The Ugandan Diaspora (or *"Kyeyo*, as I discussed in Chapter 5. This group is interested in Ugandan products and services, they use the internet alot AND they have loads of money!

3. Knowledge

Ugandans are very inquisitive - they want to know. They are looking for online solutions to their problems. The Google search results for 2013 show the following to be some top searches:

- ***What is*** - *Love, development, internet?*

- ***What is (health)*** – *stress, bloating, AIDs?*

- ***What is (business)*** – *marketing, planning, research?*

- ***How to*** – *kiss, love, bet, pray, hack?*

How do you turn this into a money making opportunity?

Consultancy. Ugandans are asking these questions, so all you need to do is set up a business to answer these questions. For example:

How to kiss, love, pray – Online counseling services.

A website where information is available on the internet and includes the option to call a specific toll free number for telephone/chat counseling (clients pay via mobile money). Affiliated services would be to enter partnerships with clinics or even shops selling products to help (e.g pills, books).

Appendix 1: 12 powerful words/phrases you MUST use in all your marketing material

Based on Chris Cardell's "break through strategies", CD, June 2013 for the VIP Inner club. In it Chris had a discussion with copywriter expert Jon Mcculloch. Chris Cardell is considered to be Britain's leading Marketing expert. Jon Mcculloch is considered to be one of Ireland's leading copywriters.

1. **How to**. People only search for solutions to problems and this immediately attracts attention. Especially works on Google and Pay per click advertising. Other variations include in telling stories, which are also powerful in marketing. "How i…"

2. **You**. It's based on the concept: "What's in it for me"- People don't care about what you do, they care about what you do for them. Use "You" in your headlines and other key materials e.g "You will achieve…" This forces you to change the focus to benefits/needs/wants of the customer rather than what you do (features of products/services).

3. **Scarcity related phases.** Words like *"deadline" "Limited number" "Special offer"*. This works as long as it's genuine, otherwise your integrity will be questioned. Don't for example use "Special offer" when in actual sense the product/service is on sale every day.

4. **New.** Other variants include "improved". The human brain is programmed to pay attention to change, particularly those that make their life better, without a lot of effort because by default we don't like change so anything promising change, we pay attention to.

5. **Exclusive**. Other variants include *"unique" "limited edition" "secret"*. We all like to have something that no one has access to. This can be used to command a premium price as people like to feel like they belong to an exclusive club for a product/service.

6. **Member.** Instead of referring to "customers" refer to them as "members" or "subscriber" This is connected to the previous one of exclusivity and helps people to feel that they belong.

7.   **Reason why.** The principle behind this is that people want to believe and can accept anything as long as you give them a reason to believe. Hence say "the reason why is because…." A scientific study has been done to show how effective this, even when people are being convinced to do something wrong or with no merit.

8.   **Fee.** And other variants like "amount", "instalment" rather than using the word "price" or "cost". How about saying the "this investment is worth Shs X to you…." Rather than "the price is". The human brain has conditioned to be defensive when the word price or cost is used so use these other variants helps break down resistance to price.

9.   **Easy.** People are fundamentally lazy and so like everything to be easy/effortless. Use of this word makes people read your material.

10.   **It's not your fault.** People don't like to take responsibility or be told they are wrong or lectured to, even if they are in the wrong e.g "it's not your fault that you are overweight, its *McDonald's* fault". Use of this phrase gives people a reason to feel better and therefore can work.

11.   **Fast.** In an ever changing world, people want things immediately and people will pay a premium for say e-books or electronic items they can get immediately rather than say waiting for a hard copy version, even if it might be of superior quality. People want immediate and fast solutions to their problems and so a promise to deliver something fast will give results.

12.   **Isn't it?** This is a "tag question". What it does is get people in the habit of agreeing with you. Once you get them in the habit of agreeing to simple things like: "it's a good day, isn't it" "we guarantee that if you do not like it, you can return this product, that is a fair offer, isn't it?" then once they are conditioned, they will keep on agreeing, including when you ask them for more business or to make a sale to them. It is based on studies done in Neuro Linguistic Programming (NLP). It is especially effective in face to face or phone conversations. Of course it can be manipulated for evil but we of course recommend it's used for good too.

Appendix 2: Business plan template

Creating your business plan is an important and valuable exercise – even if you are not preparing it to raise funding. The process will raise useful questions and help you to both plan your strategy and structure your business effectively.

The plan doesn't need to be a long document, most funders will only read the Executive Summary initially in order to decide whether they wish to find out more – in fact you would generally only present the Executive Summary in the first stage of discussions.

So we suggest that in doing the plan, Keep it Simple and Straightforward (KISS). Here is a suggested format for the plan or a layout to help you in developing your idea.

A - Executive Summary

This is a "mini version" of the plan itself, setting out the key elements of the business and proposal. The headings in the Executive Summary will generally mirror those of the plan itself.

Executive Summaries are often non confidential, whereas a full business plan may contain confidential information and would only be supplied once a Non Disclosure Agreement has been signed by the recipient.

If you are targeting a particular lender, the Executive summary should clearly outline "what you want" i.e how much you are looking for and what you are offering in return (security, collateral, shares).

B - Overview of the business

Describe the business, including:

- its products or services,
- location, a little history, why it was started.
- What is the purpose of the business and key objectives?
- What "problem" is the business is looking to solve?

C - The need and market size

Scalability is a key factor for many investors. If the business cannot be increased in size on a profitable basis, many investors will be unlikely to take things further. Underlying the understanding of the market and its needs should be concrete research both desk (ie internet and research journals) and field research (e.g surveys, discussions, observations).

- Do you intend to grow the business significantly or is it planned to be a "lifestyle" business
- What is the need for the product or service, how is this demonstrated.
- What is the size of the target market in both unit and revenue terms, include forecast market size for the next three years, split if necessary by region or country.

D - About your market

- How have things changed/are changing in the market you supply (trends e.g technology).
- What are the key drivers/economic/social/political factors which are relevant.
- How will things change going forward or in the future?.

E - The product/services and operations

- Detailed description of the products or services and plans for future products. Many funders will be wary of a "one product company".
- Describe your operational plan, how the business will deliver to customers, your team's experience in doing so.
- If your team has no experience in all the key areas, who will you bring in to fill the gaps?
- What internal controls will you put in place including for ensuring quality of products/services and for meeting obligations (e.g tax, social security, council taxes)?

F - The competition

You need to include a reasonable assessment of the current and likely future competition.
- How do their products and services compare to yours
- what is your competitive advantage and positioning in the market.
- How is the competition and their activity likely to affect your strategy now and going forward?

G - Marketing and Sales

When, where, what, timing, logic. Describe the marketing, sales and distribution strategies/plans including the experience of those involved and the likely challenges you will meet as you try to get your message out to potential customers.

How will/can you implement some of these marketing strategies below?

- *Direct mail*
- *Surveys to establish what customers want*
- *Referral strategy – how will you reward customers or how will you ensure this works*
- *E- mail marketing –how can you capture more email addresses? How can you offer free and useful information in return for emails, how can you use an auto responder to drive email marketing*
- *Pay per click advertising – Google and face book advertising, can they work?*
- *Free public relations and press – how will you use these?*
- *Networking, exhibitions, and events – give people the real thing*
- *Offer explicit guarantees e.g Guaranteed fun or your money back!*
- *Give Free stuff in advance*

H - Intellectual Property overview

A key area (if relevant to your business) for most investors. Remember that intellectual property covers not only patents & trademarks but also know how, business processes, etc

I - Risks

Discuss the risks and threats which your business faces/will face. How are you planning to deal with these – what is your plan B in each case?

J - Management team

Structure, details, general experience, relevant experience to your business, roles and responsibilities

K - Financial forecasts

Headline figures in table form for at least 3 yrs showing
- Revenue
- Gross Profit
- Net Profit before tax (EBITDA)
- Max cash requirement

The financial forecasts must be supported by a detailed financial model which includes sensitivity analysis (i.e. "what if" scenarios – what if sales fall by 20%, or costs increase by 20% etc).

L – Funding

- Amounts already invested into the business (where from, type and how much)
- Funding Requirements & likely structure/type of funding
- Consider alternative funding options e.g shares/equity to skilled persons
- What are you offering the investor in return for his investment
- You need to clearly make a compelling offer. If a loan, you need to factor in the cost of the loan (interest and repayment) into your forecasts.

M - Use of funds

- Broad summary of main areas of expenditure split into capital expenditure (e.g assets) and recurring expenditure (e.g rent, salary, marketing).

N - Exit Strategy (and maybe comments re likely valuation)

- Sale of shares?
- Succession planning?

END

P.S Some of the ideas here are from fundingstore.com

Appendix 3: Sample internal control programme

1 GOVERNANCE

Potential Risks:

- The Board of Directors (BOD) does not have procedures in place which allow it to fulfill all its responsibilities in managing the business and its finances
- The lack of clear direction results in weak governance and reduces accountability and effectiveness

Controlling the Risks:

- A Scheme of Delegation and Summary of Financial Delegation (For example a signatory list) are in place which charge the BOD with the responsibility of managing the business and its finances
- Up to date, agreed Terms of Reference exist for the BOD and its committees.
- For day to day operational matters the BOD have determined how they will delegate matters to members of management and staff
- There is a clearly set out business organisation structure, financial management policy and finance procedure at the business.

	CONTROL	STATE HOW THE BUSINESS MEETS THE CONTROL	CONTROL ADEQUATE Yes/No
1	The roles and responsibilities of the governing body and its committees have been set out in writing.		
2	The roles and responsibilities and membership are reviewed and amended as required.		
3	There is clear documentation regarding the delegation to member of staff with financial responsibilities.		

4	The documentation is reviewed and agreed by the board on an annual basis.		
5	All board members and management and staff with financial responsibilities have access to and an understanding of the Business's Financial Policies and Procedures Manual.		
6	Governing Body and committee meetings allow decisions to be taken in line with the deadlines set by the board and others.		
7	All decisions made, who has made them and what action has to be taken is clearly documented and distributed to all concerned.		
8	An up to date record of "related party transactions" is maintained of business interests for directors and staff who influence financial decisions.		
9	Procedures are in place to ensure that financial control is maintained in the absence of key personnel.		
10	Proper accounting records are maintained and retained in accordance with the document retention schedule.		
11	All accounting records are retained securely and access is controlled.		
12	There is a Policy which has been made available to all staff to enable staff to raise serious concerns regarding any aspect of the business's work.		

Based on the responses to the above what is the:

Likelihood / Impact of the risk	H / M / L
Action required	Y / N

Key:

H- High

M- Medium

L- Low

Y- Yes

N- No

2 FINANCIAL PLANNING AND BUDGETARY CONTROL

Potential Risks:

- Failure to plan ahead over several years and target resources to specific priorities reduces effectiveness, levels of improvement and potential for growth
- The business fails to manage within its available resources - at best becoming overdrawn at the bank, and at worst putting its going concern status at risk

Controlling the Risks:

- The Strategic Development Plan (SDP) will normally cover a period of 3-5 years. To ensure that resources are available to meet its objectives there must be clear links from the SDP to the business's annual budget
- Budgeting and subsequent regular budget monitoring are essential to good financial management.

	CONTROL	STATE HOW THE BUSINESS MEETS THE CONTROL	CONTROL ADEQUATE Yes/No
1	The financial resources required to meet the business's goals and strategic objectives are identified in the SDP.		
2	Sufficient detail exists in the SDP to provide the basis for constructing budget plans for the next and future financial years.		
3	Procedures are in place to allow the board and staff adequate time to appraise the likely costs and benefits of any new initiative.		
4	Actual and projected customer numbers are closely monitored.		
5	Historic spending patterns are not unhelpfully perpetuated when constructing the budget.		
6	The Board receive budget monitoring reports which are regular, informative, understandable and include commitments, outturn forecasts and variations.		
7	Bank reconciliation takes place in a timely manner		

Based on the responses to the above what is the:

Likelihood / Impact of the risk	H / M / L
Action required	Y / N

PURCHASING

Potential Risks:

- The business does not achieve Best Value
- Suppliers are not chosen impartially or on the basis of fair competition leading to a potential for fraud or damage to reputation
- Lack of commitments can result in overspending
- Quotations/tenders are not sought in line with the business's policy
- Spending via credit /debit cards is not in accordance with the procedures agreed by the board

Controlling the Risks:

- Evidence to show that the business has obtained Best Value for its purchases should be retained
- Commitments, with the exception of utilities, should be placed on the business's finance system PRIOR to the order being sent.
- Sufficient quotations and tenders should be sought in accordance with the business's regulations before any decision to purchase is made.
- The board should be involved in decisions.

	CONTROL	STATE HOW THE BUSINESS MEETS THE CONTROL	CONTROL ADEQUATE Yes/No
1	Price, quality and fitness for purpose is considered when purchasing goods or services.		
2	Sufficient tenders and quotations are obtained		
3	Board approval is obtained for all expenditure in line with authority limits.		
4	Service contracts are delivered in accordance with the contract specification.		

5	With the exception of utilities, an official pre-numbered order is generated for the purchase of goods and services (including verbal, electronic or faxed emergency purchases).		
6	Controls are in place over reimbursement of staff purchases (where personal cheques or credit cards have been used)		
7	Orders are used only for goods and services provided to the business and not for private use by staff.		
8	All orders and deliveries are authorised/checked with adequate segregation of duties.		
9	Outstanding/late orders are monitored regularly.		
10	Procedures surrounding the use of credit/debit cards are being followed and controls are implemented.		

Based on the responses to the above what is the:

Likelihood / Impact of the risk	H / M / L
Action required	Y / N

5. PAYMENT OF INVOICES

Potential Risks:

- Payments are made for goods or services which have not been received or ordered by the business
- Payments are made for the wrong amount
- Payments are made to the wrong supplier
- Payments are duplicated
- Interest charges are incurred due to late payment of invoices

Controlling the Risks:

- There is adequate segregation of duties. No one person should be able to order, receive and pay for goods and services
- Before any payment is made there are appropriate checks to ensure the accuracy of the invoice, that it agrees with the order and that the goods or services have been received.
- The person authorising payment of the invoice is sure it relates to business expenditure and has been checked for accuracy.

	CONTROL	STATE HOW THE BUSINESS MEETS THE CONTROL	CONTROL ADEQUATE Yes/No
1	Procedures are in place to ensure that what has been delivered is what was originally ordered.		
2	More than one person is involved in authorising the order and certifying the invoice.		
3	Only original invoices are processed for payment once they have been checked, coded and certified for payment.		
4	Procedures are in place, and followed, regarding the processing of electronic invoices.		

5	Invoices are certified for payment in accordance with the scheme of delegation of authority.		
6	All paid invoices are marked in some way to prevent duplicate processing.		
7	All invoices are paid in accordance with agreed payment terms		
8	Items are recorded on the inventory if appropriate		
9	Cheque runs are reviewed prior to the cheque being signed.		
10	Cheques are not pre-signed		
11	VAT is accurately calculated and correctly applied		

Based on the responses to the above what is the:

Likelihood / Impact of the risk	H / M / L
Action required	Y / N

6. PETTY CASH

Potential Risks:

- Petty cash is used to bypass normal payment procedures
- Duplicate payments are made through the creditor or payroll systems
- Personal cheques are cashed from the petty cash float
- Cash float is held in an insecure place
- Reimbursement is made without appropriate paperwork
- Cash is handed out in advance of purchase without receipt
- Income & expenditure is not recorded promptly
- The total of cash in hand and receipts does not match the agreed limit

Controlling the Risks:

- The petty cash is only available for use in emergencies or for small value items which would be inappropriate to put through the creditors or payroll systems.
- The board/management should agree the procedures and a limit above which petty cash cannot be used
- Although relatively small amounts are involved in the transactions the same accounting principles apply ie no one person should be responsible for authorising, paying out and reconciling the petty cash
- The petty cash should be reconciled at least monthly
- Any discrepancies should be reported immediately
- The petty cash should always be reimbursed back to the agreed limit

	CONTROL	STATE HOW THE BUSINESS MEETS THE CONTROL	CONTROL ADEQUATE Yes/No
1	There are written procedures for the administration and use of the petty cash.		
2	The level of the petty cash float held is appropriate to the needs of the business, and has been agreed by the board/management		

3	The cash float is held securely and access is limited to authorised staff		
4	Payments from the petty cash are limited to minor items of expenditure.		
5	All expenditure is supported by a receipt, (VAT where possible), is signed for by the recipient, countersigned by an authorised member of staff and presented in a timely manner		
6	The petty cash is reconciled on a regular basis, at least monthly.		
7	Claims for reimbursement of the imprest account are made on a regular basis and are authorised by staff with delegated responsibility.		
8	An independent reconciliation of the imprest account is undertaken on a regular basis (at least 6 monthly) by a person other than the account administrator.		
9	Personal cheques are not cashed from the cash float.		

Based on the responses to the above what is the:

Likelihood / Impact of the risk	H / M / L
Action required	Y / N

INCOME

Potential Risks:

- Charges or rates for goods/services are not appropriate and/or consistently applied
- Income is not banked in a timely manner
- Insurance limits for holding cash are exceeded
- Cash and cheques are not held securely
- Inadequate procedures for the collection and recording of income
- Income is not recorded/goes astray
- Controlling the Risks:
- Charging policies for goods/services or standard price lists are established, agreed and reviewed by the board on an annual basis
- Official, pre-numbered receipts, or other formal documentation should be kept for all income received
- Procedures exist, and are followed, for the collection and banking of income

	CONTROL	STATE HOW THE BUSINESS MEETS THE CONTROL	CONTROL ADEQUATE Yes/No
1	The charging policies as above are up to date and set out details of charges, discounts and concessions and reviewed on a regular basis		
2	There are procedures for reviewing and monitoring all income due to the business		
3	Invoices are sent as soon as a debt arises		
4	The business requests all cheques are made payable to the business		

5	All staff are aware of the procedures in business for collecting money and handing it over to the person responsible for banking		
6	All income received is recorded and receipted where applicable in accordance with agreed segregation of duties.		
7	All machines that take money, including telephones, are emptied regularly and the cash counted by two people.		
8	All cash and receipt books are held securely in a safe or fire proof, lockable receptacle.		
9	Access to the safe is restricted to authorised staff.		
10	Banking is not less than weekly ensuring that cash held is within the insurance limits		
11	Income received is not used for the encashment of personal cheques or for other payments.		
12	Income is banked promptly and intact.		
13	There is an independent reconciliation on a monthly basis of the income received and income banked.		
14	There is proof of monies collected by a security company.		

Based on the responses to the above what is the:

Likelihood / Impact of the risk	H / M / L
Action required	Y / N

8 FIXED ASSETS

Potential Risks:

- No independent record of fixed assets held within the business
- Losses are not identified if the asset register is not reviewed and updated on a regular basis
- Lack of control over stocks of materials and other consumables results in loss and waste as well as stock being unavailable when needed.
- Items are lost or mislaid, possibly damaged or stolen without recognition until they are required and cannot be used or cannot be found
- Lack of security marking reduces chance of recovery in the event of theft.
- Lost/stolen items cannot be identified/recovered
- There is no plan for the use, maintenance and development of the business building(s)

Controlling the Risks:

- A designated member of staff has responsibility for the fixed asset inventory system. This person ensures that the register/inventory is up to date
- An annual check of the inventory is carried out by someone other than the person who maintains the register
- Items 'loaned' to staff are recorded
- Items taken off site are logged out and signed back in again
- Items should be security marked with the an asset number of other identifying information
- The business's maintenance plan should work in conjunction with the annual budget and Strategic Development Plan (SDP)

	CONTROL	STATE HOW THE BUSINESS MEETS THE CONTROL	CONTROL ADEQUATE Yes/No
1	An up to date inventory is maintained of all assets above the level agreed by board and those that are deemed portable/desirable.		

2	An annual check is undertaken by an independent officer to ensure the physical items agree to the items listed on the inventory. The inventory is signed and dated to confirm agreement.		
3	All discrepancies are investigated and any over a specific value are reported to the board.		
4	All property taken off the business site is recorded, signed for and its return recorded.		
5	All write-offs and the disposal of surplus stocks and equipment is undertaken in accordance with written policies/Financial Regulations and recorded as such		
6	There is a procedure for the security of premises, it is adequate and reviewed regularly.		
7	The number of keys in existence to buildings, safes, etc is limited to the minimum practical and access to them is controlled.		
8	All keys to safes, cash boxes and other receptacles in which money or valuables are secured are carried on the person of those responsible at all times.		

Based on the responses to the above what is the:

Likelihood / Impact of the risk	H / M / L
Action required	Y / N

9 DATA SECURITY

Potential Risks:

- The business does not have an appropriate IT and data protection policy
- Insufficient or irregular password security and access levels
- System is insecure and/or individuals have inappropriate access rights
- Inability to recover lost data
- Lack of up to date data protection software
- Unlicensed software is used

Controlling the Risks:

- Set up of an IT and data protection policy
- Access to software is adequately restricted and protected
- Regular back-ups are taken, including an off-site copy
- Regular updating of the virus protection
- A Policy regarding the use of computers is in place

	CONTROL	STATE HOW THE BUSINESS MEETS THE CONTROL	CONTROL ADEQUATE Yes/No
1	Access to computers and data is limited and passwords are changed regularly		
2	Personal information held is in line with the Business's Data Protection policy		

3	A designated officer has been identified to manage the IT environment		
4	Regular backups are taken to allow rebuilding of systems. One complete back-up is held off site to safeguard against loss of data		
5	Users are aware of the need to protect the computer system against viruses by not using their own software		
6	The system is adequately protected against viruses		
7	All software applications are licensed		
8	Staff are aware of the accepted use of the IT equipment		
9	The system is kept up to date and accurate eg new starters are given access rights where appropriate and leavers rights are removed in a timely manner		

Based on the responses to the above what is the:

Likelihood / Impact of the risk	H / M / L
Action required	Y / N

10 INSURANCE/RISK

Potential Risks:

- Risk Assessments are not conducted on a regular basis, inc. Health & Safety checks
- Sums insured are inadequate
- Additional items are not added to policies in a timely manner
- Losses are not reported

Controlling the Risks:

- Risks should be reviewed on an annual basis
- Alterations to policies should be notified to the Insurer

	CONTROL	STATE HOW THE BUSINESS MEETS THE CONTROL	CONTROL ADEQUATE Yes/No
1	There is a methodology for identifying, assessing and addressing risks and documenting the process		
2	All risks are reviewed annually to ensure that sums insured are commensurate with the risks.		
3	There is a procedure for notifying the insurer immediately of all new risks, property, equipment and vehicles that require insurance or where it affects existing insurance.		
4	The business notifies the insurers immediately of all accidents, losses or incidents that may give rise to an insurance claim.		
5	Regular Health & Safety checks are carried out, with reports being forwarded to the board.		

Based on the responses to the above what is the:

Likelihood / Impact of the risk	H / M / L
Action required	Y / N

Checklist Completed by :. ....
Date:..................

Reviewed by: -...............................
Date: ………………………..

Appendix 4: An example of exceptional customer care
The cab driver ("special hire") driver with a mission statement.

A man called Harvey was waiting in line for a ride at an airport in the USA.

When a cab ("special hire" taxi in Uganda) pulled up, the first thing Harvey noticed was that the taxi was polished to a bright shine. Smartly dressed in a white shirt, black tie, and freshly pressed black slacks, the cab driver jumped out and rounded the car to open the back passenger door for Harvey. He handed Harvey a laminated card and said:

"I'm Wally, your driver. While I'm loading your bags in the trunk, I'd like you to read my mission statement."

Taken back, Harvey read the card. It said:

Wally's Mission Statement:

"To get my customers to their destination in the quickest, safest, and cheapest way possible in a friendly environment"

This blew Harvey away. Especially when he noticed that the inside of the cab matched the outside. Spotlessly clean!

As he slid behind the wheel, Wally said, "Would you like a cup of coffee? I have a thermos of regular and one of decaf."

Harvey said jokingly, "No, I'd prefer a soft drink."

Wally smiled and said, "No problem. I have a cooler up front with regular and Diet Coke, water and orange juice."

Almost stuttering, Harvey said, "I'll take a Diet Coke"

Handing him his drink, Wally said, "If you'd like something to read, I have *The Wall Street Journal, Time, Sports Illustrated* and *USA Today*."

As they were pulling away, Wally handed Harvey another laminated card. "These are the stations I get and the music they play, if you'd like to listen to the radio."

As if that weren't enough, Wally told Harvey that he had the air conditioning on and asked if the temperature was comfortable for him. Then he advised Harvey of the best route to his destination for that time of the day. He also let him know that he'd be happy to chat and tell him about some of the sights, or, if Harvey preferred, to leave him with his own thoughts.

"Tell me, Wally," Harvey asked the driver, "have you always served customers like this?"

Wally smiled into the rear view mirror. "No, not always. In fact, it's only been in the last two years.

My first five years driving, I spent most of my time complaining like all the rest of the cabbies do.

Then I heard the personal growth guru, on the radio one day. He said that if you get up in the morning expecting to have a bad day, you'll rarely disappoint yourself. He said, 'Stop complaining! <u>Differentiate yourself from your competition. Don't be a duck. Be an eagle. Ducks quack and complain. Eagles soar above the crowd</u>.'

"That hit me right between the eyes," said Wally. "He was really talking about me. I was always quacking and complaining, so I decided to change my attitude and become an eagle. I looked around at the other cabs and their drivers. The cabs were dirty, the drivers were unfriendly, and the customers were unhappy. So I decided to make some changes. I put in a few at a time. When my customers responded well, I did more."

"I take it this has paid off for you," Harvey said.

"It sure had," Wally replied. "My first year as an eagle, I doubled my income from the previous year. This year I'll probably quadruple it. You were lucky to get me today. I don't sit at cab stands anymore. My customers call me for appointments on my cell phone or leave a message on my answering machine. If I can't pick them up myself, I get a reliable cabbie friend to do it and I take a piece of the action."

Wally was phenomenal. He was running a limo service out of a Yellow Cab. Wally the Cab Driver made a different choice. He decided to stop quacking like ducks and start soaring like eagles. How about you?

About the author

Dickson Wasake, FCCA was born in Mbale, Uganda to Derrick Gafali Wasake a retired economist and Sarah Wasake *nee* Maswere a business entrepreneur.

He was educated in Uganda at *King's College Budo* for "O" and "A" Level and then at *Makerere University (Business School)* where he graduated with a Bachelor of Commerce degree (Accounting).

He then obtained a post graduate qualification as a chartered accountant (ACCA) while working for *PricewaterhouseCoopers* (PwC) in Uganda and in the Bahamas.

PwC is one of the world's "Big 4" professional services firms.

In 2013 Dickson also attended a Leadership Development Programme akin to an Executive MBA at the *University Of Chicago Booth School Of Business* ("Chicago Booth").

In 2012 and 2013, Chicago Booth was ranked no. 1 by *The Economist* in the MBA rankings. It was also ranked no. 1 by *Bloomberg Business week* in 2006, 2008, 2010 and 2012 and no. 2 Business School by *Forbes*.

Away from work, Dickson spends time with his daughter, loves poetry (he is a published Poet) and is always up for a good debate, having been a guild speaker while at University and a chairperson of the senior debating club while at A level.

Credits

To the team at Inachee who continue provided the support including reading drafts of the book. I am most grateful and in particular to Doreen Mwesigye and Joseph Walusimbi my business partners and co- sharers in the hard but rewarding days - past and future.

I am also grateful to my kid brother Donald Wasake for asking for "pocket money". I refused and instead offered to pay him for every research piece he did for me in the "field" to support the articles I put up on an early blog for the "best sectors" concept . We really started out as a two person "brief case company" with him on the streets - and me behind a computer.

To our most diligent subscribers and clients. Thanks for the support. Some of the principles included here were first shared via the "Advanced Thinking" newsletter and the feedback received from the subscribers and clients was inspiration for this – to give back to our subscribers and clients.

The cover photo is courtesy of *"History in Progress Uganda."* Unfortunately I do not have details of the photographer to whom the credit or copyright belongs.

Dickson Wasake, January 2014.

www.ingramcontent.com/pod-product-compliance
Lightning Source LLC
Chambersburg PA
CBHW021900170526
45157CB00005B/1896